MAGNANIMUS

By: Krystal Berger

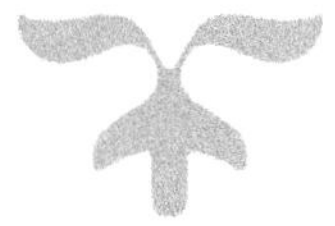

DEDICATED TO:

MR. USSERY

ank you, Sir, for your continued efforts on our journey of healing. I
will forever be in debt to you.

ISBN: 9798878123006
Imprint: Independently published

<u>Magnanimous:</u>

First let me just say

I've only begun to understand

What it feels like

For the heart to crave

Oh, mister fifty shades of grey

I'm perplexed by you

And your guarded ways

But being as though

All I have known

Is the many ways my heart has been disappointed

I can only know that I am

Guarded too, in that way.

Take me into those dark places

Because see, there with you, the depravity is

True intimacy recalculated

It's an openness created

Where the lines of intimacy and real art never hesitate

To feel a touch of want

And to watch pleasure naturally reciprocate

The beauty exists where our bodies meet

It bleeds into this unnatural to me,

And sort of effortless state

To just be open and remain unapologetically me.

It's really terrifying to feel this vulnerable

But softly seen.

Just one of those things that in ten years' time

I'll lay awake and reflect

Even if it isn't you laying next to me.

[2]

<u>Naked:</u>

Standing here naked and raw

In my mismatched

Panties and bra

And you're moved to want

To possess it all

You speak to me with intention

And all you ask for

Is a little off my attention

Excuse me, sir

Did I forget to mention

By you just existing

You have me diving headfirst

Into a craved submission.

So when I hear about

These layers you speak of

Let's peel them back

So I can embrace each one

When all you ask

Is for my time and attention

I beg you

Require more

I want to create new needs for you

That we can explore.

Sweet man I implore

Let me give you all of me

And so much more.

[3]

Speechless:

Speechless,

Left without words most days

But Some newness you gift me

And I'm baffled

Left in disarray

With contemplations on my plate.

Seeing standards

I didn't know I was allowed to seek.

Becoming in tune

With my neglected senses

Realizing truths,

Like it's been years since

I've snorted

You know a genuine laugh,

Brought on when fully relaxed

Learning the difference

Between being touched

And actually felt.

For someone to listen...

It hits far different

To be heard.

Am I Setting standards?

I beg your pardon.

But you've set a precedence

On who a man should be to me

And for that

You will forever hold my gratitude.

Savoir:

Oh love save me,

Being trap back here

Between where my mind

Keeps on reminding

And what my heart begs for

Stuck in my head all day

Making excuses

And figuring worse case scenarios

Holding my breath

And holding back

Each one of my words

Feeling stuck in a fantasy

But love I don't want to daydream

I want this to be my reality

The good, bad, and ugly.

Make it real to me.

Reassurances.

Just comfort me

Waves of sullen

Wash over as I

Anticipate an end

I'm not ready to see.

Please love rescue me

Be not another man

Simply sent in to test

Or rather ruin me.

<u>Contemplation:</u>

Sitting I contemplate

Caught In thoughts of

What futures May hold

But that is all I've ever known

Planning and pursuing

Out of my control

What futures May hold

I wanna exist right here

In these few minutes

Rewind and repeat it

Drown out the demons

That force me to stay breathing.

Sink into something new

A warmth that is

His fire that burns

His rage and brokenness

Let me get lost

In these stitches and mends

Nursing wounds

That are all too familiar to me

Lost in the waves

You sucked me in like an undertow

And it feels like my soul

Has made its way home.

So please don't tidy up things.

Don't make room for me.

Just let me be present

To appreciate this beautiful scenery.

[6]

<u>Magnitude:</u>

Excuse my hesitation

See when you

Dream of something

For a lifetime

When it manifests

You lie in a transition between

Grasping onto what is real

Versus sifting through delusion.

When I look into you

Explore the way you move.

You Laugh it off to me

"You act like I'm a rarity"

As confused as you maybe

King, please understand me.

You were crafted

Beautifully made

And scary as it may be to me

I've known of you

Longer than I care to repeat.

You were born from daydreams

Lusted after between torn pages

As mythical as the burning phoenix

A compilation of

Beautiful reoccurring dreams.

This intangible gift

Forever floating out of reach.

So please forgive my hesitation

I'm still waiting, for someone to pinch me.

[7]

<u>Exiled:</u>

In folklore

There are these things

Known as wisps

See that's what I imagine

When I feel a soul as soft as yours

Caress against this.

Statuesque in stance

But your sadness begs

You were never

Really offered a chance.

You weren't built

For a world like this

Forever misunderstanding

Your soul's purpose

See sweet man.

By design you were cultivated to

Capture, Sculpt,

And turn back out

Beauty into an

Unforgiving abyss

So to know and touch

To explore

Such a beautiful force.

To cross paths

And be allowed to exist

In a space so warm and delicate

This exchange

Is by definition a truly inspired sort of gift.

[8]

<u>Onion:</u>

You move different

Softly and with caution

Small little shifts

In the access you share

In the way you address me

Is it your confidence in me

That I see building

A comfort in knowing

This consistence is easy

Because for me it's naturally?

The easiest thing

To be soft

And love on you truly

To support and encourage

Because with me there is transparency

A reciprocated honesty

I'm excited to meet

This man

The way you are allowing

Earning privileges

Peeling back layers

I adore, that for me

It seems like it's

Coming out naturally.

[9]

<u>Big Picture:</u>

Sometimes I gravitate

Pre-plan to be consumed by

Compelled to disassociate

This I know as much to be true

Because facing myself,

Aside from mothering you,

Is too much to do.

I'm comfortable in this space

Wrapped up in you

The weight of knowing,

My purpose is not yet fulfilled,

Outside of loving you.

Left in my loneliness

Until my focus is once again you.

That burden of completing me

Should not be left on you.

My love,

I promise mommy is working on

Something much bigger than her

So when you are ready

To not need me as much

You won't have to resent me

For smothering so much.

<u>Your Burden:</u>

I hold on to the love

I have for you,

Focus on the good memories

The ones I swear are

All I have of you

But not a day goes by

You don't deserve a good

Fuck you.

Fuck you for

The demons you battled

And the fucked-up ways

you would handle them.

Fuck you for choosing the bottle

Fuck you for

sitting in those cell blocks

Fuck you for

Not protecting me like you should

Fuck you for

Dying on my watch

Fuck you

For making me watch

Fuck you for

Not being here to watch her walk or hear her talk.

But most of all fuck you

For not being here

when I needed you the most.

And for loving me

So God Damn much.

[11]

<u>Sobs:</u>

Tears are easiest to cry

When they are formed by anger

Cast in resentment, and pride.

I can rage inside

Asking all the whys

And come to conclusions

That will answer those whys.

But when facing a truth

And those more difficult tears rise

The ones fostered by

And emptiness inside.

Formed by a hollow loneliness

That is often hindered

By distractions and

Self-told lies.

It's much harder to contemplate.

To really dive in deep

And dismantle

Feelings of being incomplete

That twisting ache

Pulses in a much deeper place.

The kind of self-reflection

Most are too numb to partake.

A necessary discomfort

So you must swallow your pride

So true self actualization

Can really take flight.

[12]

<u>Yearned:</u>

Far more than a yearning

It's a deeply rooted burning

Sewn into the fibers of my being

It hurts deep down

To crave you so completely

To never be fully satiated

The warmth

That energy

Your kindness that envelopes me

Tie me up in bondage

Trap me there forevermore

Because to me it's heaven

To be imprisoned here

Amongst all your

So called demons.

My body quivers

It's shakes in anticipation

Until the moment comes and

I get to taste our freedom.

So know when I utter this

I mean it from

The depths of my very being

To be entangled with you

Every waking moment

Is a fantasy fulfilled

After a life of never having.

[13]

<u>Nevermore:</u>

There is a warmth

Tucked behind that

Half cast smile

The one you go through

the motions with

The one you use

when you play pretend

The warmth emits

From the fire within

You call it a darkness

I know it as an old friend

Oh too Familiar it is

So I understand

The tongues those demons

Speak in.

Let me lay to rest

The idea that anyway

They may preach

Will they ever beseech

Me to flee.

For I feel at home

In your layers as you unfold.

[14]

<u>Resonating:</u>

Resonating inside

Profound in its vision

The understanding

Of this wisdom

Forged within me

The pain it took

To find this joy

How low I got

To stand as tall as I do

The ugliness I was delt

To see the real beauty in me.

The violence it took

To become this gentle

The darkness I wade through

To become a light for others

Recognizing these truths

It's easier to forgive the past

Knowing how beautiful

It's made this version of me.

<u>Usurp:</u>

The softness you know in me

I need you to understand

Is who I am

Who I desire to be

Not who the world

has allowed me to be.

The warmth in which

You choose to embrace that

Is steady allowing me to reciprocate

It outwardly

Not just onto you but

Onto a world that

Otherwise doesn't deserve

A single kindness from me

Comprehension is key

Your attentiveness is bringing out

The best kind of woman in me

The idea that before

I knew your boldness

I was sinking into a coldness

And a reawakening

Set loose in me something

At first, I was scared of

But now I desire to

Simply embrace it

I hope one day you choose to keep me.

Because I know my soul

wants that completely.

[16]

<u>Glass Garden:</u>

Days have passed

Turned, twisted, flipped

Into weeks and month after month ends

In this pursuit,

My wanderlust, pursuing myself.

Loving and nurturing

Who I'm meant to be

Has cultivated this beautiful landscape

A garden of softness for just me.

Despite the crudeness

The audacity. The misspoken. Misfired disrespect

Intended to muddle this garden with a few new weeds.

The higher the fences

As I mend and recalculate my defense.

I bask in this

But don't think for one moment

I don't sit a self-reflect

Contemplating on what my worth would be

If I wasn't formed into this perfect dream

Spiritually lusted after

By men who seek understanding and how it's so easy

That I remain unattainable.

I urge you not to peer over that fence

and bask in the beauty these flowers offer.

For that wall has been refortified.

Made impenetrable.

For I was built to love unconditional

But never was meant to be loved in return.

<u>Impressing:</u>

How kind it is

You slid right in

Snug like a puzzle piece

Showing me my place

Come here

Whispered with a look

While your existence

Calms my storm

Allowing my soul a home

Here in this peace

This soft little place

Like a pillow fort

You built for me

A second home

To breathe unashamed

Of this form I've been given

This laugh welcomed

And my words listened

Intentional are those little things

The kindness you afford me.

Seek more of me

Because King, I owe you everything

For the standards

You've set for me

Simply by being that X, Y, and Z

Every day you

Impress me effortlessly.

[18]

<u>Acid washed:</u>

I've circled back

To this place

One in which I concentrate

On those most toxic traits

I have value. I know my worth.

But why is it I second guess

A kind man's intentions

Why is there a heaviness

Upon my chest.

When I feel like I'm steady

Always waiting for the shoe to drop

Why do I ask?

"Why does he want me?"

Is it really as easy as this?

What are his intentions

Please hurry up and hurt me

Get bored and drop me

So I can get to moving on again.

Start over and once again improve myself.

Lingering here in the

Well I know I'm worth it

But does he seek me

Or is this self-serving?

Why do I plague myself

In reflections and hesitations

Is it not knowing my true value, Or is it self-sabotage

Because it's easier to step in my own way

Then to know real love and loose it.

[19]

<u>Unsure:</u>

I am unsure

How many times

I've started to type it

Or typed it and deleted

Too scared to know

What your answer would be

If I sent it

And you chose

to be honest with me

A million times over

On any given day

I ponder over it

Try to make guesses

Thoughtfully calculate.

It paws at my heart.

And sometimes I feel

So when I do

Muster the courage

To break down and

finally send this.

I hope you decide

You will be honest

In your reply to it

But why is it me?

Is it me you're really after?

Or am I a place holder

Fulfilling neglected fantasies

[20]

<u>Effortless Asset:</u>

I crave you

Not of flesh, but to keep you

To work on myself to be the best I can for you

See very rare is it that prayers are answered

But ironic it is how things can be spoken into existence

I once remarked,

"I'm tired of little boys, Who can only bark, Insincere in their advances,

Who only seek validation, In the responses of women."

Tired of games played and the disrespectful

Way they would waste my time.

And when I began

To fold my hand

My gaze set upon

The in every way right kind of man

One who just wanted me, sought my time.

Illiterate verbally, but it was beautiful

Because he was incapable of finessing me.

Not a fuck to give about how anyone perceived him.

And every little thing he did

He moved with intention.

Effortlessly with effort

This man swept me.

Moved me and grew me

Watering in ways I don't believe

I even knew I needed

So when I say, I would gladly spend

A lifetime returning the favor

I mean that with every ounce of my being.

[21]

<u>Self-proclaimed Reprobate:</u>

Be still, Hold in this moment

I want my love to soften you

Just enough from within

That you for once, you see your own value

Understand you aren't like them.

You are as rare as a precious gem

When I found you

The odds where a billion to none

Simply unfathomable, Hun.

You are a game changer,

Abundantly meant.

Your heart not meant to be understood

It speaks in languages

Most won't comprehend.

Just know that is because you aren't meant

For just any of them.

Your darkness is a place fires rage in

That passion is not a weakness, flaw, or a sin

See yourself a villain

But most of them were just superheroes

Whom most just didn't understand.

I could list all of the ways you are the best kind of man.

But for now, let my love soften you

So one day

you can really comprehend.

When I finally find the courage

To say the words

I've only been showing with actions.

[22]

<u>Known:</u>

I wanna know you

As deeply as

I do my own reflection

I wanna trace

Every shadow you cast

And I wanna dance

Amongst every word

Spoken to you

That's intent was

To point out some

Made up inadequacy

I want to hear

Every lie you were told

And every one you spoke to yourself.

I wanna greet each one of your demons,

Converse so deeply

I leave knowing them

by middle names.

I wanna explore

Every tick,

Every still healing sore.

I want to dive so deep into you

I forget how to breathe

Because when I

Finally come to the surface

I want to earn the privilege

To be the first to

Love you correctly.

[23]

<u>Reserved:</u>

Man of few words

Moving about

In a world that was not meant for you

Different in the way you move

Hardened by mistreatment

Not given the right

Kind of chance at living

But when you take me in.

There is a softness in you

And unspoken understanding

You know I am worth keeping

Forgive my aggressions

My attempts at provoking you

To move with intentions.

For I know you are deserving

Of the love I am capable of giving

And you are absolutely

Worth keeping.

To do right by you

My only duty

But my frustrations

Are demands

For you to let me

In just a little more.

To give me the

Opportunities to pour

Fill your cup King

That is really all I'm asking.

[24]

<u>Slowed:</u>

Slowed, paused in this moment

Our warmth collides

And atmospheres realign

Our bodies pressed

And amongst the heat

We form a diamond

This beautiful picture painted

Tears and soft moans

Bleed between the lines

Exhilarating

Captivating

Nothing more than pure bliss

Is ever presently cultivating

As my moans hush

That is when it hits

Simply put

it moves me

Every time your body

and mine entwine

we create a delicacy

That the Gods will forever envy.

<u>More:</u>

The more I want

To drown myself in you

The easier it is to pull

Myself away from the world

Fill my cup and pull all of me

Right back in

So I can truly give you all of me.

It is the least I could do

In reciprocating

All the little things

You may not realize you do.

This is the hardest

Because I know

What this does to me

Leaves me careless

Deluded with the idea

I am just carefree

Twisted up in a fairytale

Or A contorted daydream

I have never craved so much

A place with someone

So calm

So welcoming

I can just be.

And that be enough

Just to exist.

In the spaces between

The ticking of our time.

[26]

<u>Powerful Silence:</u>

Oh the power of silence

Hurts like a gut punch

But I did it to myself

Moving a way I was not meant

Showing a face

In an ungrateful way.

Or so is the route

I feel this has taken

But love my intention

Was merely to encourage

To allow you to set boundaries

Say to me, "I just need A minute."

Let us reset. Let me focus a bit

But the silence when you chose to step away

Echoed loudly and shook

The world around me.

An ache I felt in your absence

Give me if only half of you

And here I will sit and wait

Please kind to me

My heart was not built to withstand your silence

Tell me I'm crazy, tell me to back off

Put me in my place

But please don't leave me

Trapped with my own thoughts

On an empty stomach.

While part of me

Is silently missing.

[27]

<u>Pretending:</u>

Let me play pretend

Close my eyes

When I am by myself

Imagine you here with me

The little things

Cooking in the kitchen

Imagine you staring

at me from the table

With that little smile

The one that encourages me

To just do my thing

Let me play pretend

When I look over

Into that empty passenger seat

Imagine that road trip

Just vibing to whatever

Playlist we shuffle through

Smiles and laughing

Flirting across the console

Let me play pretend

Visions of you

Taking my hand

In those moments

You see me getting worked up

Calming my storm

With that soft smile of yours

[28]

I am the type of woman

Absolutely confident

And comfortable in my peace

But please dear man

Excuse me while I take pause

And bask in this

Not sure what you have been doing

But the way you have gotten me moving

Has gotten me off balance

Little more than stumbling

Catching myself doing things I did not know

I was capable of

See, it is a special kind of thing

A different kind of feeling

So use to planning for just me

And I am steady daydreaming

Of all the new memories I want to be making

I have been photoshopping you

Into my daily routine

Images of you staring

Back at me from the kitchen table

With that little smile

Encouraging me to keep

Just doing my thing.

Or the flirting across the center console

While the white lines zip bye

And RnB is steady playing

While we both sing off key.

[29]

<u>Simple:</u>

Simple as,

In those moments

I start to get worked up

I have started closing my eyes

And breathing

Imagining you taking my hands

To calm my storm.

A bucket list my mind is creating

Of all the moments

I want to spend with you.

I hope to make it all

Feel like Deja vu

Getting lost in life

Experiencing it all with you.

But if I am perfectly honest

It scares the shit out of me.

Sincerely,

A woman who is not sure

Exactly what this is.

Just loving the chance

To get lost in it.

<u>Perfected</u>:

Perfection may not exist,

For the world is torn apart

And no one is meant

To be everything all at once.

But for me, In my world.

Perfection does exist.

I have grown to

See, understand, and appreciate it.

It is hidden in your smile

When you laugh too hard

At your own jokes

It exists in the space

Right between where

Your fingertips and my skin kiss.

It is in the very tone when you choose

To allow my name to cross your lips.

It exists in the way your mind spins about,

And the way you hold Yourself to account.

The times you bathe in self-doubt

For fear you are not

A better man

Day in and day out.

So to me perfection

Very much does exist.

Perfection looks at me often

And says, "I am just me."

You, mind body and soul

Are the perfection that has my heart weak.

[31]

<u>Boundaries:</u>

I ponder

Lost in thought

Trying to grasp onto

What this may be

The little bit in the depths

Eating away at me

Stress from day to day

Or a guilt

Steadily chipping away

Am I selfish

Or no longer afraid

To ask

And seek

Setting boundaries

For days

Weaving in and out

Of the fuck it's

And it'll keep for another day

Inching my way along

Seeking new purpose

Am I only just okay

Or is that a lie

I tell myself on the surface

Just to wake up

And fall in line

With the daily circus.

[32]

<u>Broken rules:</u>

Throughout a life

Seeking myself through entanglements with men

Finding my purpose and an understanding

In what it means to be loved

I got caught up seeking

Something I could never find in any of them

On that journey

I was met with little regard

Always being done to Never for

Was usually a place I had to separate myself from

So I would feel less like a whore.

No matter my intentions

Having to separate myself mind from body

To play my part, because that was what was required

To belong to one of them.

Then I met the in every right way type of man.

Who showed me the way intimacy

Should be performed.

And it's a beautiful thing in which I begin

To embrace my own form.

Found my grace between breaths and a divine suppleness

With every touch He grounds and centers me

Never more present then when he thrusts into me

Creating a longing that this flower yearns for

Watering me daily.

So for you, rules are meant to be broken

When everywhere you kiss me

I feel a little less torn.

[33]

<u>Purpose divine:</u>

See, sometimes

When getting to know me

The saddest part happens to be

The most beautiful thing

Inside of me

My desire to give

To love, To nurture

Despite the cards dealt to me

I've always known this

So I accepted the hurt

Of which it associates

Because I love

That kindness inside of me.

If I am honest in this speech

I never knew it would become so liberating

To meet this purpose and have it met

With such adamant forces

To watch a soul grow

In trusting my actions

To be fielded requests,

I remain eager to meet each one of them

For it fills my heart so absolutely full

It burst with notes from a melody

Written with every letter of your sweet name.

So please never stop

Giving me direction to these places.

I would fight currents

To meet you in every damn one of them.

[34]

Packed House:

The amount of men

I have encountered

Who wished to speak to me,

be in my presence.

To shoot their shot.

To spit their game.

Coming at me with their best foot forward.

Easily over a hundred men.

I would never keep count,

Not even task myself

to remember

Even half of them.

This my love I do know

of them

Not a single one

Had the superpower

To make me melt

The way you do.

Soften me so effortlessly.

Tap into the core of me.

Make me nervous and simultaneously relaxed

into the safest space

I have been blessed to know.

Not just in a room full of,

but in a stadium full of men.

My heart would seek you

Hone in and find you

Despite every fucking one of them.

[35]

<u>Absolute:</u>

Absolute pressure

Does not begin to define

Or even

Have the opportunity

To draw the lines

For the very man you are

Passionately blind

Unforgivingly redefined

Even at glance

The heavens

Where shaped by

The intensity of your eyes

Gods shaped mountains

Based off the form

Of your very body

When you speak

It rumbles almost godly

Your smile burns

into one's soul

brighter than

every star in the sky.

So absolute pressure

Is merely an insult

To a man

who's very stance

Defines the very word

Devine.

<u>Tidewater:</u>

When most women

Venture into the world

What they are taught

Is what they know

From years of being told

That this is so

These expectations and

Those standards of

What a man should hold

They tend to seek out

A partner and then allow

Their mind to decide

If he is the man

To bring her the moon.

Throw a lasso around

Bring it in close.

And on those conditions

She swears

For him she would die.

But for me.

It has never been that easy

I have spent a lifetime

My own value never enough.

So in this

Your comprehension is key

For you I will exist,

For you, my intent is to live

If your intention

[37]

Simply is

Not to bring me the moon

But simply exist as it.

Bring me light

In my darkness,

Lighting my way in the night.

For heaven is far easier

to see at night.

Not a thing is required

But for you to linger here

Simply exist.

Exist as you are.

For your light is warm.

And there isn't a thing

I would not do

To remain wrapped up in you

So, don't underestimate yourself.

You lull nations at bedtime

You influence the whole world

Not just it's tides.

<u>Penmanship:</u>

All I have known

Is to be hushed

To be left to my own

So in that silence

Stories would unfold

Daily ignored I was

Always overlooked

And deepen the meaning

Of which these lines

Would one day hold

Polishing the pen

And with words

I would befriend

Because outwardly

I knew I would

Be alone in it

So page after page

Setting it down

To then, years later

Picking back up again

Never does it betray

But it encourages

And often enough

It liberates.

To be good with words

Is a blessing

That being silenced

Gave to me.

[39]

<u>Allow me:</u>

For a moment allow me to be cliche

Reference the old

To bring perspective to this new form

You are gifted to hold.

For Greek Gods

Understood the beauty

In bondage and suffering.

To know suffering

It's been an endearing friend

Not so much a foe

For in me it crafted an empathy

So intensely bold

In bondage

I was held to

impossible standards

My emotions laid bare

As days turned into years

Those chains shifted

I grew to know a peace

But in it minimum efforts laid bare.

For drifting, not living

Was what ensnared.

Now as I am laid bare

Here before you

In these ties and binds

For me it is paradise

Set free and living

In the moments between sighs.

[40]

<u>Weeded:</u>

Many things I've learned

As days turned into months

Falling into the start of years

Self-realized.

Harboring growth

My heart has healed

And in many ways

Much stronger for the pain

I've known

Exhilarated I have grown.

Like a weed ironically

Because it was without love, little support,

And almost in despite the conditions

Of all the things I have learned

And of the things I understand.

I know me well enough

To know if I ever lose you

I would never want to meet you again.

Never look for you In another man.

Because realness,

Beautiful in its rarity,

It is something meant

To be appreciated

And valued daily.

And should I be

The reason we ever depart

I do not deserve another

Chance at this reality.

[41]

Let me make this

Abundantly clear

I will never not want what we have here

For my body bare

Has never known a warmth quiet like this

Your resemblance

Stays dancing in my head

And my body reacts

Lusting, in need of it.

So much so as I part her lips,

She begs to borrow your tongue, so she can better articulate

how much she craves Him.

As if trained by Pavlov

She salivates at the mere

Mention of it.

Her decadence is only meant

To be savored by the most righteous of men

And for her she will serve

A much deserving King

Embrace my curvature

As you let my taste dance across every one of your taste buds

Beckoning her, to play for you

So that when you decide

To hush her wanting cries

Parting my soft shaking thighs

And you do begin to thrust

She will take hold

Hugging like she is afraid to get lost.

<u>Gifted:</u>

I promise I am doing my best

And if it was not for you

And the doting way

You proclaim, "Mommy you are the best!"

My mind would eat at me

On a daily basis

I am sorry for the way

I over explain the actions I take with you

I am sorry I'm not better

At hiding bad days at work

from you

I am sorry in the moments

I am short with you

Raising my voice

Because it is the third time, I'm repeating it to you

I will always remind you

I love you, you are enough, You're beautiful

And each day mommy is trying

To be her very best for you.

Just know that through it all

Your smile, your laugh, your "mommy is the best"

Is what keeps me from thinking

I am never enough for you.

Because for me, my love

You move mountains

You reshape stars

You are the very reason

Some days I get up in the morning.

[43]

<u>Stricken:</u>

It slips out

I know, most often

In the way I look at you.

You can hear it

In the soft sighs

When I get caught up

Getting lost

Staring at you.

I could spend a lifetime

Rearranging every word

Spoken by man

But not a sentence

Could come together

That would do justice

In defining the presence you are

So for now

I ask you to take up every

Unoccupied moment in a day.

Take up every inch of

Free space in my mind.

To play the lead role

In every dream

I watch at night

Be the substitute for

The air I breathe

But most of all I ask

Keep being the version of you

Who is you, unapologetically.

[44]

<u>Description:</u>

I could describe it

Much like an ache

But that's not quite right

For when you aren't with me

It's the same as

That nagging feeling

Like when you

Forget to pick up something

While out shopping.

Or when you left the house

And feel like you

Left a light on.

Like something is missing

But you can't place your

Finger on it.

For I'm not in pain

In your absence.

Because I'm certain

You've grown to be

An important part of me.

But rather things

Tend to matter less

I don't feel as complete

Until once again our eyes do meet.

In that moment

My heart feels whole

Like my soul

Has made it back home.

[45]

My wish one day

Is for you to be able

To reach into my chest

And feel it

Feel what it feels like

When I think about you

For a minute

A tightness and tingle

Like an excitement

That is calm

But meaningful

That stir in deep inside

Like your soul was just lifted

That is what you do

You exist

And it feels like

All of my insides were

Simultaneously kissed

It brings about a yearning

But not for the explicit

But rather to give

All of me to you

Laid out for you

To do with what you see fit.

It is like free falling

But knowing with everything

There isn't a bottom to hit.

[46]

<u>IT</u>:

King when I say you are IT

I mean

Everything a man should be

About his kids.

Fighting against a world

Who doesn't want to

See him come up in it.

You are accountable

Sure of yourself

Unapologetic and comfortable in your weirdness

You are laughter and you are pain

You are strength outside of it

You are preserving

You are inevitable

You are a force to be reckoned

And a healing presence

You calm storms

But have a fire that rages

You are encouragement and kindness

A hood dude with manners

A protector, A provider

Ever growing and masculinity redefined

You are beautifully melanated

And a king whom with every breath

Desire is satisfied

So I hope that helps in understanding

what I mean when I say

Handsome man, you are absolutely IT.

[47]

<u>The Warmth:</u>

The warmth

When you pull me in

My gasp

Upon your entrance

Like it is the first time

All over again

Unexpectedly anticipated

Longingly lusted after

Even more so

It is what my heart does

When our eyes meet

And I see your smile

shine back at me

Excuse me

For around you

I am a deer caught in

Headlights

Your presences just

Blazes so beautifully.

Let me get my bearings

And remember

All the things

You taught me

I am capable of doing

Words I know

I Understand them

I Can rearrange and

Play with them

Make just about anything

In any situation fit just right.

But when I am with you

I find myself

Stumbling

Stuttering

Tripping over my own breath

It is the whole way about you

That when I am around

And caught up in you

I just want to shut up

Sink in and adore you.

I just want to

Move well and serve you.

I want to be so delicate,

With my touch.

I make the flesh

Your soul is wrapped

in feel like it's been

hugged by the heavens.

I want to satisfy you

So thoroughly

You feel gluttonous

And overweighted

[49]

But in a single breathe

Like your whole world

Has been lifted.

When I speak these things

I sing them into existence

It is absolutely imperative

That you understand.

What I say without saying

The things I leave unspoken

Are not because I wont

Acknowledge their existence.

Just didn't know my heart

Would be so eager to receive this

Because my King, I promise

what I understand is.

You are just you and

I am merely reciprocating.

And it is okay to leave

Certain things unspoken.

<u>Convinced:</u>

Often times I convince myself

that I am all right

I can do it by myself

But honesty is truth

Truth is my policy

I was fine all by myself

Until I saw a world capable

Of more than what it has ever been.

I've realized that

Not a day goes by I don't crave you,

Every part of my being

Built to never want to say that I need

In my heart though

I know that I desperately do want to need you

And as each day passes,

I feel a dependency

Start to creep in

Between the sheets

Of this intimacy and it is scary to feel like

I wouldn't be this me without you.

I hesitate and I know

It is not that I need it proven or shown

Just needed the time

And few wrong moves

To reassure me that.

I do not want to be me without you

So cheers to me for letting myself fall

Head over in trust with you.

[51]

<u>Fly on the Wall:</u>

If you were a fly on the wall

You would know

With all certainty

The truths I know

That my heart beats

To the rhythm

Of your melody

That my lips enjoy the taste

Of describing all that is you

That my mind has reserved space

For shelves upon shelves

Of your images.

That my love language has shifted

In a way

to best cater to you.

And that inside

My demons rage battles

Against what my heart wants

And with what past selves

Deemed me worthy of

That since you

I have a comprehension

That loving myself

Has become another way

To even more love you.

If you were a fly on the wall

Sweet man

You would have no doubts at all.

[52]

<u>Timid Girl:</u>

She was timid

A people pleaser

With good intentions

A boss babe

And confident in herself

Consumed by surviving

Because no one

Really had her like that

Until her eyes were opened to

A special kind of life

Approached and whisked away

By a beautiful black knight

He Showered her with effort

Redefined consistency

Liberated her from within

Showed her the strength

And all of that beauty locked within

And effortlessly with a grin

That man unlocked a next level kind of bitch

Unsure of the intent

She sunk deep in

Moved to study

Understand, serve

And love relentless

For that black knight

Rescued a damsel

Who didn't know

She was distressed

[53]

<u>Baring Fruit:</u>

My heart beats

And sometimes it is enough

To just breathe

But never will I be okay

With not being

Who you need me to be

For the universe

Chose you for me

Not because it would be easy

But rather to build

A better woman out of me

To cultivate and hone

A part of me

I didn't know was worth loving

Child of mine the love you give

Is beautiful and unrelenting

When I am unfair Or just plain mean

With all sincerity you muster the courage

To love me anyway your love is the first

I have known to be truly given unconditionally

I know this home I have made

Is far from conventional

But being in this space with you

Makes it a home in which it is worth living

So let us sing our hearts out

Speak with our whole chests

Let us be bold and grow together

Learning to put ourselves first.

[54]

<u>Fumbled:</u>

When days turn to nights

And the bad days

End in smiles

The thoughts that linger

Have for a while.

How could a woman

Even half the value

Fumble a man

So completely filled with value

From the gentleness

In your smile

To the firm standards you hold for yourself

The encouragement

That pours from you

To the accountability that stays wrapped

In your fists

See when I look at you

Just know, your existence just fits

Like a missing piece

You just are

And I feel complete

For me, the very man you are

Is just it.

So here is my apology

From every not quite queen

You were tasked to encounter

Sorry they fumbled you

Because King, I absolutely do see your value.

[55]

<u>Playoffs:</u>

In this second half

I find the score board

Is all tied up

But I have never been a quitter

And going into overtime

Is not always an option

So making this second half count

Is an absolute must

Going all in to

Make a better life

And live for us.

See when you play yourself

Long enough

The plays develop a pattern

If you pay close attention

You can predict

your next step

So we learn to redirect

Go for that Hail Mary

In hopes better days

Take risks

Love yourself

Because battling yourself

On the field

Is a hopeless endeavor

You are always bound to lose.

<u>Instructions:</u>

I do not always know

The right thing to say

How to play a role

Or how to operate

With no instruction manual

But one thing is

For certain

As long as my heart beats

I am in it for you

I am willing to fail

And start all over with you

Drop the ball

And pick it up

Chasing finish lines

I am not even sure you drew

Because the thoughts

Of a silence

I would be trapped in

Without thoughts of you

Are a hell

A damnation

I would not wish upon

The worst abomination

For when you have touched heaven

Every place after

Feels like not quiet home.

[57]

<u>Burning it:</u>

You are IT

I did not know at first, I was not sure

My hesitations,

Based on a feeling of being cursed

But the more you remain.

The more certain I am

Of what is behind this burn

Three little words that are hard as fuck to murmur

You are IT

You are a cool summer storm

The kind where you let the water hit and caress your skin

While at peace you stay dancing in it.

You are IT

A refortified levee, against my own undoing

Showing me how to battle my own demons

You are IT

Because you exist despite every place you have been

And you choose to be this version of you for me.

A queen who has never been loved right

Never felt seen.

You are IT

Is the substitution for what I really mean to say

Which is

I am madly,

In head over heels,

Absolutely and truly.

Well what I mean to say

You are IT.

[58]

<u>Moved:</u>

I feel moved to

But quickly I hush myself

To ask more of you

With all the effort you give

But it isn't moves

It is conversations

The ones I avoid

I have reservations

Who is she for you?

And your intent on me?

I just want to know

Where I stand baby.

Reassurance is the thing

My mind is craving.

Does she wake up next to you

Even though she hasn't

Been so deserving to

Do you think of me

When you kiss her

Am I a fantasy

An escape from responsibility

Or do you play a role

To satiate her?

I have concerns understandably

I was someone's wife, once too.

<u>Something in the blue:</u>

See the best way

I can articulate

This feeling inside

It feels as though

A cold numbness overtakes me

Starting at my fingertips and slowly creeps

It's way inwardly

Like driving in the winter

With the heater on and the windows down, and a sleepiness

Renders your body

But a little slap on the cheek

Does not work to wake me

Just have to ride it out in hopes it does not take hold of me

Just focus on my breathing

Distract and keep busy

Best way I have learned to prevent that emptiness

From consuming me.

For pity is not what I seek

Just be kind and patient and understand that

Not a thing you could do would do this to me.

Do not take this momentary blues at all personally.

That's the only thing that would hurt me.

For this to make you feel any less deserving

So bear with me while I reserve part of me.

Because somethings just aren't fair for you to see.

[60]

<u>All In:</u>

I wanna be your rock

I wanna be your peace

I wanna be every one of your fantasies

I wanna be everything

That the ones before me failed to be

because when I look at you what I see is a king

who has never been met

where he deserves to be

Someone so kind and loving,

the best kind of man

who deserves all of me

Absolutely Deserving

sometimes I think

I am not quite worthy

I want to be the one

on whom you lean

I wanna love you with all of your demons

all of your shortcomings

I want you to know that it is OK to be

exactly who you were meant to be

I don't want to ask anything of you

just that I can be for you

and allow me the space

to love you completely

Tell me how you want me

because if I am honest,

One thing I know

is that you absolutely complete me.

[61]

<u>Exceptional</u>:

When I happened upon you

My heart hunkered in fear

Tampered down

Amongst thickets of razor wire

Prepared to shoot first

Ask questions later

Do I even dare

But I was caught off guard

Not knowing miracles could exist

To get lost in

A peace like this

To not have to fight

Prove I am enough

Just exist and have someone want me as is?

Effortless

Shameless

More so how could it be

That a man like you

Just is?

Better than good

Rather exceptional

Like when a rainstorm first hits

And everything thirsting

Is quenched.

All I can say is

Thank you for this.

Because of you

I know heaven exists.

[62]

<u>Existing:</u>

I want to exist between thoughts

I want to feel more than

Just what I feel in a moment

I want to know what it's like

To trust those feelings.

Having been gaslit so long

I have to convince myself

I am not losing it.

Don't want to ask

Just to be met

Somewhere kind

For the sake of it.

I don't want to have to share

Or beg and wait for attention

Don't need it constant

Only consistent

I hurt myself daily

Waiting to see what

May come of it

Why is it I'm only seen

And it's only kept men

Who put in the efforts.

What does that even mean?

How fair is that to me?

That get their needs met

While I unlock a door

To my empty residence

Night after night

[63]

No warmth in my bed

But I chose it?

Fell for one who

I can't be sure actually cares.

Maybe, he wanted his needs met

Finessing is casual

And undressed I laid bare

I give all but part of me

But it's merely meant to kill

Kill off that part of me

That would hope

someone would care.

Hoping to break myself

Entirely of trusting a soul

I do know, you see,

I Teach myself lessons repeatedly

To make sure I know

Back there is where

We will never be.

So I'll keep giving my heart.

Give him every last bit

Because once this ends

I don't want to start over again.

<u>Internal:</u>

Sometimes I want to scream

"No one said sorry to me"

Sometimes I want to drive

With no destination in mind

Between you and me

The demons I fight

Are not battling me

Or some misplaced guilt deep within

They fight daily

Against what I let happen

To younger versions of me.

You see

My rage is eternal

Because there are

Too many faces haunting me

Not a single muttered apology

Every kick was while I was down

And I smile

Despite every face of evil

I was dealt.

And in my silence

My smile beams

While those voices scream

"Not a soul will care if you wake up tomorrow"

And my darkness stays

Alone, hugging me.

For my ghosts are not

anyone's burden to carry.

[65]

<u>Space:</u>

I want to take up space

Respectfully I crave

To watch you exist

In any give space.

I beg to be

Something profound

Someone motivating

Respectfully I crave

To adore all that you are

To have part of my purpose be

To remind you

of who you are

To instill a kindness

And love without

Any kind of conditions

Just be that softness

That brings out the best

The kind that upon touch

Your whole body feels at rest

Respectfully I crave

To make loving me back

Seem sort of effortless.

[66]

<u>This Part:</u>

I think this part

This is what's hardest

Having wants

Stumbling over needs

Ones I know

Myself I cannot meet

To rely so damn heavily

On if I am good enough

I am not a chore

I will forever sing

But damn why is it

That past whispers

So fucking loud at me

Even though I never was

That difficult you see and I know this

But something in me is broken,

maybe damaged internally

It is not some self-righteous

Confident reason I won't be tasked to beg or plead

Eternally for me

It's a fear that if

I fixed my mouth

To ask for something

They would just disappear.

So suffer in silence

Through self-learned fear

To speak a want

Or be left looking in the mirror.

[67]

Yes sir,

A newly acquired mating call

Let me earn the privilege

To service you

And your every beck and call

Allow me to

Savory every inch

You feel the need to serve me

Let me feel you run down

The back of my throat

Watch me drip for you

As my pleasure

Is in serving you

Yes Sir,

My moaned response

As I follow your request

Following your lead

Because you know what's best

Fold me inside out

Don't hesitate to

Play with me

Anyway you see fit

For a King gets what he needs

And service should be

At his request.

<u>Forgiveness:</u>

Please forgive my stares

See when with you

I try to take it all in

Imprint your image

Deep into my soul.

Forgive my stares

Because sometimes

I'm still in disbelief you exist

Somehow it cannot be real

Forgive my stares

Because in those moments

Words do not work

To justify the admiration

And gratitude I have

For such an amazing man

Forgive my stares

I am just trying to lock it in

For the real bad days

I am able to close my eyes

And teleport back here

Forgive my stares

Because I have never had

Someone like this.

Someone who just is.

Forgive my stares

But I am just dumbfounded

On how effortless

You make loving you is.

[69]

<u>Intimacy craved:</u>

What I crave

Is a rom com meet cute

Because if I am honest

I grew up knowing

I would never be cute enough to

I want to dance together like no one is watching.

I wanna get caught up

In a summer rainstorm.

Let's play pretend just for a minute

I want to sit at the end of the bar

And let you buy me a drink

To turn down

Your first shot.

I want to be chased.

Have someone make

Me a mixed tape.

Never knowing what it's like

To be a leading lady.

I wish I were the woman

Who was captivating

Upon first glimpse

But I stay knowing

You'll first have to

Talk to me a bit.

I wanna hold onto knowing

Romance still exists.

And it isn't sitting across

From you at the Chilis on 5th

[70]

<u>Smitten:</u>

I am sorry for my intrusiveness

But I can only admit

It was harmless

Then you spoke and

I admittedly became smitten

After that first kiss

I knew this would be dangerous

And all of a sudden

I became lost

Caught up and seduced by it

With every hit of your soft smile

Like Novocain

I float higher

With every spoken word

Of encouragement

My need

To meet yours

Simply renders me breathless

With every intentionally caress

I fall to my knees begging for you

To be the one to ruin me.

I've chose this submitting

Because your heart

Is what truly makes a King

So I am sorry

For my intrusiveness

But thank you for

Letting me get lost in this.

[71]

<u>Broken Little Girl:</u>

Caught in a whirlwind

The only love language

she's knew of was violence

Left alone her plight

Alone with the fights

Alone she cried and on her own

Figured out how to navigate life.

Stumbling through stages

Blindly searching for a light

To see a flicker

Reach for it and watch as it was

snuffed out before it grew to bright.

So in a panic hands out

Aggressively searching

Hoping for more.

She wore herself down

Until there wasn't much more.

In an exhausted breath

She drew back and took a deep breath in

And realized at last.

"Flames can't be put out if I'm the one protecting them."

So inward she turned and with the violence she learned

A fire started to burn and soon it engorged.

With this she took off like a storm

Lighting the way for

A dozen more

Lost in the dark

Just as broken and torn.

[72]

Shaken Road:

I am shaking

To my core

With anticipation

What is this

The role I have taken

Every step diligent

Every right move

Hoping I make it.

Done the very right way.

Harder not easier

because for some reason

That is my nature.

Holding myself to standards

No one else sees

Since day one

Just needed to be more

Cuz what I was,

Would never be enough

Never thin enough

Never pretty enough

Never dulled down enough

My very tongue offended

No matter how soft the words

I let roll off of it.

My brain built

Just a bit different.

To only see problems

And be moved to fix them

[73]

Left alone with long enough

That reconstruction

Focused its way inward

So along with their

"You just aren't enough"

And this

"Always under construction"

Mentality

I've become

my own worst enemy

Tearing myself down

And rebuilding regularly.

While steady at work

I gaze out the window

And watch others enjoy

Succumbed to being

Blissfully ignorant

And incapable of much.

Self-awareness is beautifully deep.

But it's the only thing

That constantly haunts me.

<u>Lovesick</u>:

I know I'm lovesick

Dopamine fiending

But fuck you

Because I've never gotten

To enjoy this feeling

Toxic at best

He's on retainer

And it's a situation

We deal with

And I'm sure he'll

Turn out like the rest

But for once let me enjoy

Feeling leaned on

Respected

Dreamed of

And wanted.

Let me feel like me just being

Is enough

And I don't have to search

For it bunch of miles away.

To get lost somewhere

Along the interstate

Just let me breathe it in.

Don't worry I'll know when

I need to shut down again.

But for just right now

Shut the fuck up.

And just let me feel loved by him.

[75]

<u>Pearly Whites:</u>

Oh the beauty in your eyes

In photos they seem lifeless

Like your mind is adrift

But there is a magic

A certain new sparkle hits

When that door opens

And our irises kiss

My favorite time to see it.

Like life decided to refill them

That warmth when you take me in.

The way they fix themselves

On my lips

Like they are hanging on for life

Where each word sits

When I lay up under you

They undress my heart

Searching so greedily

To breathe in each emotion.

Reaffirmed by every kiss.

The beauty in your eyes

Is the notion I get

That I'm the reason

The light up like this.

<u>It Is:</u>

It is Him

The one my heart seeks

The one my soul needs

A balance to me

Quieting the storms

Cultivating this peace.

It is Him

My heart begs

And cries for.

In the quiet between

Where our conversations

Start and finish.

It's Him

The man in the mirror

And the one casting

The reflection.

Every form I am

In need and want of.

It is Him

Not the formulated versions

Everyone else requires,

Nor the scraps left over

When everyone else

Has had their fill.

It's the good and bad

It's all of Him

It is Him I crave

Between each breath.

[77]

Fear is beautiful

In its darkness

In one hand it can

Render you useless

In the other

Can fuel lifelong progress

In every version of me

I think the easiest to fear

Is letting myself love

Not because of fear of failure

Not the fear of getting left

What I fear the most

About love

Is one day not being enough.

For you to decide you're bored

And instead of letting me go

Putting me in a box

And tucking me

In the back of the closet

For my soul, My passion, My heart

To give all of me

To be forgotten

Disregarded

Then discarded

What I fear about love

Is knowing one day

After I give everything

I still won't be enough.

[78]

<u>First Love:</u>

The first love

A woman ever knows

Is that of her father

This set her capacity of compassion toward men

Sets her expectations

On how to receive love.

Broken promises

Lies caught onto

Fuels her capacity to love

With or without condition

Setting the bar so to speak.

So when you blame bitter women

Understand men created them.

Not ex-lovers,

Not forgetful, ungrateful boyfriends.

Or abusive husbands.

Men who were meant to protect

And guide her failed her

At the very beginning.

[79]

<u>Because of you:</u>

It was ingrained

Deep into my soul

My very purpose

To be a safe space

For men to be heard

To feel justified

To feel love despite.

The first sign of emotion

Was the night

I said goodbye

Outside of that

Was the rage and venom

That let's be honest

We're difficult for you to hide

Bottle after bottle

Hidden amongst the bar fights

A man trying to

Regain control

Of what was supposed to be

his life

A man who fought everyday

To prove he had it

He was enough, right?

Stoic and a fighter

Hiding behind pride

A scared little boy

Who just wanted his daddy

To say, "Boy you did alright."

[80]

<u>Why Is It:</u>

Why is it

Those tasked to do right

Suffer the most

And most often suffer alone?

I know personally

I never asked to do this alone

But from childhood

I've been surrounded

And on my own.

Everything is much harder

And your moral compass

Won't allow you

To put someone else down

Even if it's unintentional

So why is it, the burdens we carry

The darkness we bury

Chases us unkindly

And with unnecessary fury?

I've never hurt a soul

For self-gain, nor to get my own

Never put someone else down

To feel myself more.

I've only ever done for and that weakness

Leaves me alone.

To lay by myself

Because what is more?

My needs to be met?

Or my ethical net worth?

[81]

<u>The life I live:</u>

The life I live

The air I breathe

There are million things

Of which I'm grateful

But one thing is most for certain

This feeling in my chest

When I take pause

Take a moment to rest and take in the beauty

That is, When I watch a man

One with few words

Busy moving about this garden

Of which so many overlooked

Just weeding, And tilling,

Planting seeds and watering

Not much was here

And even still more you cleared

As if when you happened past

All you saw was the potential there

The effort was all it took and a promise I will make

That even in your absence

I will continue to tend it

With the same amount of care.

Because with the certainty in your eyes

It was made abundantly clear.

That with time an oasis will one day lay there

So thank you for the effort

Thank you for showing me

What was always meant to be here.

[82]

<u>Thoughts That Keep Me:</u>

Thoughts that keep me

up at night

What if I was the first girl

you fell for

With the heart you have

and what empire might

Lay before us

What if I were the

second woman you loved

Where would life have taken us

Anger seethes, But only occasionally

When I think of what it could have been

And how soft your heart should still be

How I've never known a man's love

And yours was always taken for granted

Who would we be if life had been more kind

And let me find you just a few years sooner

How I could have saved you

From every evil that made you

But now we sit here

As you protect me from the same coldness

That you swear overtakes you.

I wonder if the longer you hold me,

If I might be what you need to deice the veins

Running through your purposeful body.

We may never know,

But I figured you should know

Those are just a few thoughts that keep me from sleeping.

[83]

<u>Parenthood:</u>

My heart burns

And my chest tightens

A lump takes root in my throat

As I hold back

Storms of tears

Often, I ponder if I am enough

Questioning myself

And if I'm moving

Well enough for the both of us.

But this love I have

Is fierce

It rages fueled by fear

Creating a home

A safe space for us

Relearning myself

And teaching myself new stuff

Reminding myself

That the best version of me

Will always be enough.

So with each moment spent

And each nail hammered in bent

I take my time

And remind myself

That the questioning

Is exactly why I am enough.

<u>The Easiest:</u>

I promise this part is easy

Comes absolutely natural

Because when someone

Is starved long enough

They only think about eating.

I've never known of trust,

Felt valued, seen or appreciated

The only place I've felt secure

Is lost in work

Because that is the only place where respect is reciprocated

I've never known what it felt like

To not be needed

Used or beaten

Never the one

Just a blessing,

Or momentary place holder

My soul is strong

Because of how long it's felt

Weighted

So when I look at you

All I know to do

Is feed into.

Because I see a soul unappreciated

I see a kindness

Unmediated

I see someone like me

So easy to love

It would be second nature.

[85]

<u>Let Me:</u>

Let me be, exist here

And you will see who I am just is

And my heart does bleed

But the softness I offer

Isn't given to just anybody.

For who I see deserves nothing less

Than to be seen, to be loved,

To be celebrated, and Needed

For me to even breathe

It isn't what you have to offer

It's your character

Who you were meant to be.

Effortlessly about your effort

An unapologetic King,

Let that shit sing.

So loud that the echoes make stone walls ring.

Absolute pressure and the definition of masculinity

Because you redefine it's meaning.

For who I see

Deserves nothing less

Than to be seen, to be served

To be respected, and needed

To rule empires as a King.

Let me be,

Exist here until my presence

Validates everything

About you

That we both see.

[86]

<u>Irony:</u>

Ironic it is

That through this time we've spent

How deeply it hurts

To get to know

And embrace your brokenness

Juxtapose my warmth

And your darkness

But somehow it balances

And in this place, I find peace

Within the tangles

Of your brokenness

My heart heals

In its nervousness

But forever I long

To pick up your pieces

With kindness and love

Carefully reassemble them

And show you the gift

That you constantly give

To make whole a King

Whom with all the worlds cruelness

Was unkind to his loving spirit

So hold on for a bit

While I get to business

And continue to mend

Your beautiful brokenness.

[87]

<u>Silence Them:</u>

How does one quiet demons

The ones that whisper

And plant seeds that devalue

How does one rise above

And become someone

Worthy of the risk

How does one vault the comparisons

To gravitate into a higher state of being

To be believed

To be trusted

Full disclosure

I've never wanted to let someone in closer than this

To ignore every internal cry

That warns me

How dumb a move it is

But to know

Everything you are

Is worth ignoring

Every one of those excuses

Some Call them red flags

Others learned from experience

But you my sweet

Have shown me nothing

But good intentions

Shown me warmth

When you easily

Could have none to give

[88]

<u>Take Pause:</u>

Sometimes I take pause

And reflect on

All the ways I am in awe

Of the man you are

The kindness you show

Your gentle spirit

And the light you glow

It's warm

Which only baffles me

When you speak on

A coldness that overtakes you

Hinder me breathless

Kind soldier

That is what you do

When I sit back and watch

The very ways you move

Smooth conversationalist

With few words

But anthologies spoken

With a few glances

It's romantic really

The way your intention dances

Amongst the constellations

I get lost in when I fall into those irises

Speak nothing to me, King

And watch as I move

As if on strings

For you.

[89]

<u>Butterflies:</u>

Some of the most beautiful flowers

Bloom amongst thorns

And the most valuable of riches

Sunk to the depths of the oceans.

My heart aches

In waiting

But the peace I know

When I see you again

Well worth

Momentary heartbreaking

The anticipation

Like tensions build

In the days leading

Think that's why

The butterflies overtake me

So very easily.

<u>No Secret:</u>

No secret

Let's be honest

My inability to not overshare

Is why it's so easy to read me

Often, I wonder and

Never bring myself to speak on it

But why was it me

What exactly did you see

I have thoughts

Questions and some feelings

But bringing them the attention

That they seek

Has me battling

Because bringing up anything

Made me feel a problem

That needed a remedy

And often times

The quickest fix was to

Up and leave me.

I'm good at convincing

Myself that I'm healing

But is it really

That I've found a way

To hurt myself

To prolong this wonderful feeling?

Denying myself

Reassurance in pursuit

Of the noble undertaking

[91]

Of protecting your peace

Or is it that

I Know if I were to ask

For truth

That's exactly what you'll give me.

Or if I speak it will be

My own undoing?

So many places I go

To avoid that feeling.

But steady it grabs

It pulls at me.

The idea that I'm not deserving

And my brokenness

Is too unappealing

The battle that pulls

and pushes me

Is the argument

That I'm either right or wrong

In what I'm assuming

And that I'm not worthy

But I am deserving

I should share what I'm feeling

But that burden is unfair to you

So I'll keep dealing

Whatever the outcome

Of my internal monologue

My deepest fear is

I will be right

And apart it falls.

Unicorn:

To be an idea

Or rather a mythical creature,

Is rather peculiar at times

A concept foreign enough

Will lead doubters to take to stride

But those with a little hope

Will sink in to watch the show

Mesmerized and perplexed

How beautiful creatures

May actually exist

Some I warn

Will watch on

Merely to pick it apart

And convince themselves

They were right.

That such things do not exist

But know this

When the whole room is cleared

One body will stay and sit

Absolutely captivated and bound by astonishment.

So whenever the idea may decide

To flood your beautiful mind

To saw off your horn

And gallop like the other horses.

Remember these words

And know that there is always

Someone ready

To believe in unicorns.

[93]

<u>Conditions:</u>

Conditions

Those you see

By mere definition

Set any situation up

For resentment.

So know one thing

No matter which way

Your energy swings

Who you are able to be.

How much you can offer me

I am unmoved

For I need not a single thing

Just for you to be

The only expectation I have set is

For you to know peace

For your heart to be touched

For you to feel

Needed, respected, and loved.

And if of these things

Any of them

You feel missing

Lean on me

So I can put together

The missing pieces

Cuz for you

My loyalty is destined

And my love will remain

Without a single condition.

[94]

<u>Poetry</u>:

Song writers

Play writes

Poets and authors

Have written and spoken at length

In every single language.

About the beauty of love

The pain it's holds

And shaped your mind

Into daydreaming

Of what it consists of.

But what a gift it is

To be taken back

With a twist of events

To have the eyes of a romantic

And to fall in love with a man

Who sees no significance

In the spoken tongue

But rather inverts your world

And within silence

By mere action

Show you exactly

How real love

Is to be painted.

[95]

<u>Men's Value:</u>

I've lived a life.

Watched and observed All throughout it

And of all the things I've learned

The most misunderstood is what makes a man good

A good man takes responsibility

And ownership of what is his.

He shoulders pain

No one ever should

A good man knows his darkness

and although scared

He still embraces it.

A good man needs

But never asks for it.

He puts others before himself

Even though he was never Tasked with it.

A good man stands tall

While the world with all its weight

Climbs up his back

To find its place to sit.

He seeks righteousness

Before honor

Is humble and,

sometimes careless

Kind despite his

Capacity for violence.

A good man is many things

But he rarely is

Seen, Loved, Or respected.

[96]

<u>Closing Blinds:</u>

I closed all the blinds

Locked all the doors

And as I began to turn

I heard a knock at the door

Annoyed at first

I opened that door

And his eyes met mine

The tensions eased

Peering at me

A smile broke across his face

And oh how I melted

Like softened butter

Left out on the table.

My mind raced

To lock back that door

As questioned were raised

But my heart

Held my face

And promised it would be okay

Because he was different

I could feel his hug

Without an embrace

And I could smell

His warmth desperate to be taken

Oh kind stranger

How little did I know, How much it was,

That before you,

my soul wasn't at home.

[97]

Competition:

When he says I miss you

But mine says I can't wait.

When he says I'm happy for you

But mine says I'm proud of you

When he says your pretty

But mine saves every photo I send

When yours kisses your forehead

But mine says I like how close this feels.

When yours forgets your birthday

but mine records the footage

When yours doesn't listen

but mine recalls more than I remember

When yours does the little things

but mine is absolutely everything.

This is by no means a competition

Just know that

I'd rather you not

Compare yours to mine.

<u>Just Not:</u>

Everything I was not

Was drilled into

My prefrontal lobe

Like a repeated lobotomy

I was never

Quite enough

Thin enough

Pretty enough

That's all before I was old enough

For middle school

Never did get old

See because after that

I just wasn't

Smart enough

Rich enough

Capable enough

My value has always been

Determined by someone else's clock

And that I was never enough

To be loved, to be trusted

To be worth a fuck.

Not my doing

But what others worked into me

Everything I am

Is because to someone else

I wasn't So I became

Everything no One wanted

To be to be.

[99]

<u>Battles:</u>

Hard to battle with self

When self-awareness

Screams through each thought

Piercing them with brutality

When compassion

Wrestles with morality

When need talks over

Want and what your deserving

Fighting misgivings and humility

Trying to not ask for more

Than what you are giving

Treading that line of giving inches

When anticipating the miles

That could be taken giving chances

When hope is barely hanging

All while trying to not

Set expectations

Based on someone else's short comings

Navigating blindly

Being asked to trust so freely

When every move you make

Is being questioned.

Living by double standards

Set by others and fighting your urge

To believe you are enough.

Living daily in the hell I create

Wondering if it's me

I'm gaslighting.

[100]

Time's Cruelty:

Time is cruel in its honesty

Being a secret

To every man who

Ever knew me intimately

Living between the crevasses

Being loved on conditions

While fighting the voices

Balancing intuition

And opportunity

Fighting myself daily

Inner demons dropping bars

So profound

They resonate lyrically

Knowing what the past was

And who I was in those moments

Mishandled not a fault of my own

But truthfully it was

Not knowing my own self-worth.

And holding onto to hope that someone might

Actually want me.

But where is it I draw the line

In giving grace

And allowing opportunity

Standing up for me.

See, for someone to love this hard

It isn't given freely

And to lose it

Means to cut off a limb metaphorically.

[101]

<u>Womanly</u>:

Oh to be woman.

This is a task is not for the faint of heart

See guided by emotion

We are intended to be soft

That's where a man's need,

Desire to be a protector should start.

We love hard, We love first

We love despite being hurt

Told it's on condition even though we fight

Our gift of intuition

Forever at the mercy of men.

See, we have to wait for them

We have to care for and nurture them

Despite never knowing

If we are just a steppingstone

For some woman with bigger tits.

A good woman's burden

Is to be a wife without a guarantee

To prove we would be worthy, to be everything

With no promise of them choosing not to leave

To love fiercely

That we fight to keep

Instead of ever having to chance loosing.

Knowing no matter what

We are fated with the inevitability

That we love creatures

Whose clocks are just built different

And have much shorter life expectance.

[102]

<u>Rarity:</u>

The rarity of good women

In these days...

The wholesome ones

Who just want to see you happy

Despite her own misgivings

her own flaws

Her own fears

To know this love

A ride or die

One who don't play about you

Ignored all the stares

One who smiles at you

Even when you aren't looking

In awe of your potential

Never asking of you

Just to be met somewhere

in the middle

See in a world of audacity

And entitlements

These beautiful women

Steady get slept on

Now we screaming

They just don't exist.

Even though, what some of y'all forget

Is unprepared men

Are the reason for

Their abrupt extinction.

[103]

<u>Not Falling:</u>

Falling doesn't feel

To be the right adverb

More like tossed headfirst

Cuz see it was unexpected

And naturally forced

As if I was pulled on

Drawn to you.

Fought with every ounce

Because why should

Anything good ever happen

To be met with such

Thoughtfulness and intention

The respect that was given

let's not mention

How easy it was for me to be comfortable

Despite the butterflies nipping away at the inside

of my stomach

Place you in a mirror with my eyes

For just one minute

How easy it is to love a man

Who isn't easily gotten

One who's misunderstood

Absolutely underestimated

Unapologetically calm

Who understands himself

So yes, I didn't fall

I was absolutely pulled

Into the depths of heaven.

[104]

<u>Daddy Issues:</u>

It's easy to say

That every part of me

Deserves to be inflamed

Full of rage

But my heart can't

Just be that way

For every crude way

Every misused and abused way

The masculine have taunted and torn away at me

Heart broken

Lies told to, made to feel crazy

While being kept a secret

Had my sense of self

Completely obliterated

Some look and stutter

"She beautiful, how could anyone ever, simply not love her."

But to understand me, is to know

The only real love I've been shown

Was by a broken man

Who showed me how awful

But also how righteous a man can be.

The kindness despite

Their unruly capacity for violence.

So know that upon approach

No matter how much

I am able to love

I will always hurt me

In the process.

[105]

Monologue of People Pleasing:

Humble yourself,

We forget that sometimes

When we compare ourselves

To those around us.

And we forget

That just isn't good enough

Remember how it was

The only way we knew,

How we grew up?

Stop for a moment

And remember

You aren't capable of

being good enough.

You haven't done enough

Are you being of service

Or are we asking too much.

Don't get it twisted

We won't lie and say

You are simply lazy

That would be crazy.

Just sit quiet

Humble yourself,

And remember

You aren't capable

Of being good enough

[106]

<u>Mommy Dearest:</u>

We don't speak on

The silent way

The good single mother suffers

The anxiety and sacrifices

So common place

For her to face

It sucks her into it being

A natural state of living

The not enough time in a day

The nights alone, The I'll do it myself,

The last minute trips

The ungratefulness

The way she is never enough

And she needs to do better

The taunts from others never as loud

As the inner monologue she faces

The pain she feels.

The smiles she fakes

Laying her head down alone

Night after night

Touched out but craving

To be wanted and not needed

Just once.

The holidays alone

Wondering where she may have

Made that wrong turn.

Surrounded by memories

All while forgetting who she is.

[107]

<u>Motivated Isolation:</u>

Very rarely do people speak

On the loneliness you create

When all your life

What you invest

Is in the hearts of takers

And when the day comes

To put a foot down

And work to become

That healed version of you

And everything surfaces

That you knew to be true

How silent that lonely is

When you put yourself first

And have to burn that bridge

How even though,

You were always there

Now those same faces

Meet you with blank stares

When all you ever wanted

Was someone like you

Who wanted to be there.

And how painful

The realization is

That we did this to ourselves

Created an isolation

Through misguided motivations.

<u>Here We Are Again:</u>

Here we are again,

My love, I will write and rewrite

Until one day you understand

Could have been any other, but you were planned

Not mine, of course

I mean you were wanted

But there was a much easier course.

See had you been a son

There may have never been a divorce.

But other plans needed to take their course

So a little me was formed and through this

I was riddled with anxiety

How am I supposed to teach to be

Something I am not yet capable of being

See once the newness and congratulations died down

Something happened in me

That was quite profound, and it will never be

Your job to fix or protect me

That work has been done internally.

Because what you deserve

Is every opportunity given

To be silly, sweet, feminine

To be strong, smart, independent

To be inclusive, kind, and patient

And not all of these things was I ever given

So to become the best version of me

Means you will be given every opportunity.

Even the ones I'm still working on creating.

[109]

<u>Angel of Peace:</u>

I think you recall

Once I penned the line

That I wanted to be

The women of your every fantasy

And that is very true

But let's expand upon

What that really means boo.

I want ever nasty thought

To play out between us two

But also, I want to be

That place you seek refuge

Lay your head

And just know every thought told

Is concealed as if

Spoken in confessional

Emotions validated,

Denoted, and allowed

To serve their purpose.

In this peace I desire to bring

My only goal

In my efforts of being

Every one of these women

In every conceivable fantasy

Is for you to feel heaven

And know

Not a single one of your demons

Makes you any less deserving.

[110]

<u>All The Ways:</u>

Of all the ways

Our bodies

have entangled

Gotten caught up in

Lost in

The new positions

And ways I've been bent

I must confess

The most aroused I've been

Was simply in your presence

The thought of you

My foreplay

Imagery of your smile dance

And almost bring me to climax

The way you worked

Your way in

To Aline so perfectly

With my essence.

So pardon the way

My eyes soften and tear

While I'm underneath you

And my gaze adjusts

To bring you near

My body is just desperate

To become a part of you

And domination

Just so happened

To be on the menu.

[111]

<u>Love:</u>

Love is not something

to play with

Throw around nonchalant

In that is responsibility

It's work and effort

It's a heavy concept

So it's impossible for me to take lightly

So when I speak on you

The various ways I see you move

Often, I speak on demons and brokenness

Your darkness I acknowledge Because if I say you're perfect,

It will make it that much harder for you

To believe that a woman could love so completely.

I acknowledge your flaws,

Not to point out what is wrong

But to admit that I understand

The imperfections that you

Believe exist.

I know you think you may be imperfect

I love you regardless

Of who you are in light and darkness

It doesn't make you any less deserving

Doesn't take away from

Who you are as a man and if all I can accomplish

Is to lift you out of that dark

My soul has found its purpose

In loving unconditional

Without being taught how to do it.

[112]

<u>In a World:</u>

In a world that

Is not designed

With your best interest in mind

Unloving, unapologetic, unkind

There is a place

A space

I assure you

Will heal the mind

It's rare to find

But know that I'm setting it up

Remodeling a custom fit

For a man I call mine

Let it be here

In this place

You seek refuge

imbibe selfishly

For who you are to me

You deserve every bit of me.

The softness

The servitude

The encouragement

And the belief in you.

For good men exist

But you King are

Far more than them.

You are everything and more

Absolutely It

[113]

<u>Womanhood:</u>

What a woman is

Can be easily defined and recognized

What a good woman is

Much harder to explain

So let me redefine

The expectations

You have had in mind

A good woman is capable

Feminine regardless of the presence of a man.

Strong and independent

But soft in all things

That require her nurturing

And her experience

She is uplifting and encouraging

Patient and graceful

Practices tact.

Sensitive but, in control of her emotions

Sentimental and appreciative

Keeps her circle small

Because attention to detail

Means quality above all

Convenes in silence

and seeks guidance

But decisiveness her power

Accountable in all things

But above all

Her capacity for love

Is her greatest superpower.

[114]

<u>My Thoughts:</u>

My thoughts

Turn forward and back

Kind of like rocks

In a tumbler

They shuffle and get scattered

I feel overwhelmed sometimes

And my heart races

While a panic takes over

Other times

As the same stressors take hold

I breathe in

And a peace takes hold.

The momentary place

In which I'll save it for another day

Calms every single one of my nerves

But more often my heart races

<u>Journey:</u>

Sometimes I speak about my journey

But I wonder if sometimes

It's better described as a destiny

For all the right pain

And all the perfect trauma

The character it's built

Has set me on a course

To do something far greater

Than past me

Could have dreamed

For how I quantify success

Is not in what I've acquired

But the impact I've made

On those who've inquired

My heart is big

Despite its beatings

And my story, although sad

Its triumphs are worth repeating

Sharing parts of me

Almost therapeutic

Almost a sort of remedy

Working to mend parts of me

So I can teach others

How loving yourself

Can come so easily.

[116]

<u>"Just Being Me"</u>:

Unintentionally

Just being yourself

Oh how you've healed parts of me

I didn't know were broken

Unapologetically

Just being yourself

You lifted and an encourage

Gave me strength to

Go through with it

Saw a light in me

And dusted off the glass

So I could shine more brightly

Just being you

Never knew Kings existed

That could lead so effortless

Just being you

So nonchalant how you say it

But you just being you

Should me all the reasons

I'm worth loving me

Gave me a stronger hold

On my purpose

Just being you

Brought out the best in this woman.

Hearts beat

Rhythmically it seems

Sometimes slow and soft

Other times like a rave

As lightening courses through them.

The only man in existence

To choose the very verse my heart sings in

See you can soften the way my beat swings

Or light it on fire

Making the beat step two times

Just with the presence You make.

You impact my soul significantly

Control and tame me.

With the way You whisper a word

And it caresses me.

Even with no strings

I'm tangled in you

Tossed about

Between Melodies

You pen with the way

You carefully handle me.

Effortlessly

It's romantic how sure you make me

of myself while lost blind in it

Knowing with every bit of me

you're never not in control

I never knew a love song

Could be so kind to me.

[118]

<u>Along My Journey:</u>

Along my journey

Often, I hear

Where are you from?

I wanna know how

I can get me one like that.

I smile and nod politely

But here is the deal

In abundance we exist

Good women that is.

See women who chase

Are the ones

That want what a man has

Not who that man is.

Makes it much harder

To find the good women of Grace

We are found in the park

With our kids on the weekend

We are at the gym

After work

Not caked up with makeup

We are at the grocery store

Wandering in produce

Not in frozen foods

We always look focused

Maybe a little sad

But our smile lights up a room

In the back row at church

Because we don't

[119]

Want to be noticed

If we miss a weekend or two

Not at the bar chasing shots

On a kid free weekend

Because what matters more

Is our kids coming home

To a house just a little cleaner.

We are everywhere

The sad part is

Often, we hide

Because of the men

Who fumbled us

The way to win us

Is through

Honesty and consistence.

Always made me wonder

Was the original sin

Eve eating of the apple?

Or was it that

Adam couldn't stop her?

Sometimes the struggle is real

A battle within

With everything I feel

But every day I get up

And do my best

To grow a little

Love I'm sorry

For the days I'm short

Sorry for the days

I'm a little too long winded

Sorry for the way I seem

Always a little

Too self-critical

Sorry for the apologies

And my constant overthinking

The quiet spells

And how sometimes I close in

Because I'm a little

Too overwhelmed.

Sorry that I ask for patience

Just know my love

My heart is big

And for you I'd give

Everything I am

To make sure we good.

And I'm sorry for this apology

Signed a struggling:

Woman, partner, and mother.

[121]

<u>Dipping:</u>

My heart dips

It sways and dances

Under the light

That the kindness

Of your eyes

Cast on me.

It beams with

The lumens of

Ten thousand suns

With the pull of

A million moons

And not a place

I'd rather be

Then wrapped up

Under you

Caught in that

Magnanimous,

Magnificent gaze

For a peasant I am

In the presence of

An ambitious King

Gift me with your touch

Complete me with your taste

My body dances effortless

As you shift my soul

Like each of the moon's phases.

[122]

<u>I'm Sorry:</u>

I'm sorry

Odd to hear me say

But love understand

These few things

The man I know

Is absolutely worth loving

So please accept these

Apologies

You never did receive

Sorry for the way

They never did love you correctly

Sorry for the way

They used and

Always misunderstood you

Sorry for the way

That their insecurities

Blocked you from blessings

And how they

dismissed your value

Sorry for the way

You got cheated out of

Being seen and appreciated

But most of all

I am sorry

For how I wasn't ready sooner

How I wasn't there

So you wouldn't have felt

All of those injustices

[123]

Sorry that the world

Forced us to struggle separately

Sorry for not being there

In the times you most needed me

Sorry for the all the pain

That has us still healing.

I know I'm my wildest dreams

From the start it would have been

Just you and me

But I would like to think

Maybe in another life

It was only ever

You and me

Dancing together

In our own

Rhythmic melody

<u>I'm Gonna Talk About It:</u>

The first exchange of words

Prompted by a post reaction

How effortless the conversation my mind was taken back some

And how consistent

How persistent you were

Be sure to know

I will always talk about

The day we met like a Super Bowl win.

How natural it felt

To slide my fingers between yours and to talk for hours.

Smiling so hard that when I left my cheeks were sore

Every day since

Learning more and more

Watching you open up, even grow

And for us to want more.

This whole year

A whirl wind of peace, joy, and comfort

Every bit the man you are

Effortless and for you

I am not a chore.

Compels me to give and be

More and more.

Thank you for every moment

Of the past 365

Because to be honest king

You always gift me

In the way you heal me

Simply by quietly and effortlessly loving.

[125]

<u>Never Easy:</u>

I never said I would be easy

I'm not for everyone

I will also warn

That I won't ask for anything

But that doesn't mean

What I need is nothing

For what a woman like me seeks

Is effort, respect, and honesty

Don't bend the truth

Because you think it's easy

Respect wears

Many different hats

And some of that means

Creating a space

Where I can drowned

In my own vulnerability

And any thought of me

That leads to action

Will surely impress me.

Crazy to think

Because as easy

As this is to write

I promise a hundred men

Failed to meet the mark

One thing is for certain

With our effort

You hit the bullseye

Every damn time.

[126]

<u>Sickness:</u>

It feels like an illness

Like a new strain of virus

Taking over me

Ravaging my body

That is the idea of you

The thoughts consume me

In when I think I'm free

Here comes the body aches

The steady chorus

Of my body screaming

It's really tantamount to agony

Waiting for the next encounter

Just for a hit

Like a dope sick fiend

When those eyes embrace

And my body

Is lifted to another place

The moments in between

Waiting for

The end to these fever dreams

But with all of that

When again we finally meet

My heart finds peace

And I can finally breathe.

That's what I mean

When I say in passing

You are who I'm missing.

[127]

<u>Consistence:</u>

The anthem you sing

"I'm just being me"

The most beautiful way

To serenade, you see.

For the love You bring

And the way that you feed into me

Without effort

That's a King worth serving

And as you sit on that thrown

I want nothing more

Than to watch you thriving

For your best interest

Is where I'll be striving

The way that you love me

Like a gift

I will multiply, box it up

With a bow on top

And gift it back times three.

Because for who you are

And all you've been through

The man you are to me

and for me

Is deserving of all that I bring

And if you ask

If I Fuck with you

I promise you one thing

I will redefine

what that really means.

[128]

<u>The Paradox Created:</u>

The paradox created

By existing

As the kind of woman

Whoever begs for romance

Or grand gestures

Always hoping,

Never to receive them.

I will never slow dance

In the kitchen

Not pretty enough to be posted

Never the one to lean on

A Christmas Day,

By the tree, proposal.

Or to receive a kiss

When the clock strikes midnight

I'm everything to any man

With his senses intact

But not enough for the extra effort

Because I was never meant

For the ones with it all together

Forever picking up the pieces

Fixing all the broken parts

Left behind

By less deserving women.

Fuck the conundrum I've created

It's just nice to feel for once

That I do maybe matter.

[129]

I am structure

I am paradise

I am motivation

I am intimidation

I am softness

I am discipline

I am ambition

I am everything that makes

The average man great

I am the melody

That reminds you love exists

I am the whisper

That begs you to stay

I am the comfort

That urges you to live in the grey.

For when my light warms you

That's when the colors take

Twist and start to saturate.

Regardless of the life I bring

I understand

Your life is not one I can save

But hold on to hope

That this form I take

Gives you the strength

To step the way required

To become someone great.

[130]

<u>Pushy:</u>

Please forgive my pushy ways

Forgive the way

I press you

For your time

The way I require

Your attention

And inquiry

About your intention.

The soft part of me

Needs you completely

The harder parts

Want you to complete me

If it wasn't you

Not another man

Would I choose

Because it really can be

That easy

For someone to

Just want you.

To be better

When they ride for you.

I speak this with confidence

And I don't mean

To be pushy and rude

But for me

It's my truth.

[131]

<u>Plagued:</u>

A thousand questions

And a few more

Plague my brain

I wish for you it were easier

I wish for me

I could just ask these things

But I know I don't

Want to hear the truth

Because I'm happy here with you

So I stay selfish

Exclusively not giving access

Hoping That things will work out in my favor

Praying I don't

Make myself a clown

Trusting and hoping that intention

Isn't for you to have it all

While out of love I suffer without.

I know it's there

But am I just a plaything

You see my value but

Would you ever dream

Of giving me a ring?

Not that I want that

But it's not even an option

If knowing all this,

Am I the one being toxic?

Wish you'd answer my questions

Without me asking.

[132]

<u>In My Nature:</u>

I feed into

Wildly I'm unhinged

When I find a soul worth

Pouring in

So I'm sorry

For what I do

Drain myself loving you

Honestly, I don't mean to

But it's this thing

I can't help

It's that engrained need

To people please

And for some reason

Not a soul alive

Genuinely means to reciprocate

To stay giving back into me

I make it easy never asking

For a thing

I just always assumed that

If that wanted to...

But I guess they never will

Some don't try at all

Others start out real strong

And once they get comfortable

On one side it turns

The curse of meeting needs

Despite my own In hopes of feeling loved.

[133]

<u>One Sided:</u>

Transparency and honesty

Are only ever received one way

It is expected to be given

In a free kind of way

But to receive and be received

Is like pulling teeth

To voice a need

To be met

To be seen

Judgements cast

From the cruelest of place

From childhood

Voiced in cries

We learn to hush

And cast over with lies

Make things look nice

And the older we get

The more set in our ways

The easier it is

To be met with hate.

But we continue to test waters

Despite an ever-present fate

[134]

<u>Hope Enough:</u>

I hope to be enough

One day

To be woman enough

Kind enough

Nurturing enough

To be tactful

Well received

To be everything

To just somebody

Who knows how to love

To receive and feed into me

With intention and care

To be enough

More than just some

Just to be

Wanted and be

More than enough

To set aside differences

To be fought for

Protected

Adored

I'm tired of doing

Never to see it

Voluntarily returned.

I hope that

With all the words

I've spoke

Typed out

And recited

Give you an idea

Have proven my devotion

I know words are only that

For a man who only acts

But the way I move

Designed to reaffirm

And prove

I question myself

Every once and a while

If the energy I give

Is still received

And I'm feeding into you

The way you deserve

Just a little reassurance

That you are still in pursuit

That I'm still enough.

Sorry to remind you

That through my confidence

All my growth

I do still have insecurities

Sorry to ask you

To speak

And put my mind at ease.

[136]

<u>Needy:</u>

Who am I to ask anything

Of anybody

To seek love

Even if it's untraditionally

I do not see my self

Special or spectacular

That imposter syndrome

I struggle with regularly

It feels delusional to think that I am deserving

Or to think that I am able to ask for anything.

Who am I but a person

Doing my best to protect my peace

I get sad sometimes and often feel lonely

But I keep myself busy

So it doesn't eat at me.

Because not needing, only being needed

Is the only love language I know intimately

So excuse my hesitation

When a man like you shows any kind of interest

My first thought is, "What can I do for him?"

Who am I destined to be.

My fear is I will lose

This version of me

I have crafted a version of me

That for once is happy.

Please be kind to me.

I'm just a simple girl

With very few needs.

[137]

<u>That Look:</u>

Oh that look,

The way my name

Escapes your lips

Like the best

Part is to be caught up

In thoughts of me

Really know how to

Make a girl

Feel like she really means

Something more

Like the others

Were just there

But I'm real support

I'm the kindness

That gives you hope

The nurturing spirit

That helps you grow

The love without condition

You know you've always deserved

Or at least

That's the kind of title

I hoped I've earned.

Movement:

The way you move

Speaks like

Iambic pentameter

Not a word

Softly spoken

Just bold gestures

And my heart screams

For a single word to be uttered

But blankly you stare

As if urging me to stay

Blinking in Morse code

An S.O.S

Sent to just feel heard

My sweet, be patient

You are something almost new

I have to learn

But for you

I know for certain

My heart intensely burns

The kind heart of an invisible man

Found a sort of

healing type of lover

So this dance

Is strange and new

Let's just exist here

In this embrace

Of a soft, Beautiful and

Kindly warm space.

[139]

<u>Connecting:</u>

Connecting with someone

Is often a scary thing

You have to slowly

Expose your vulnerabilities

And start to trust

If you plan on building anything

This is the same

For every new thing.

But why I pause and reflect so diligently

Is because this fear is not the same old thing

Not a worry of

If you are gonna like this version

I am presenting

Not if we are going to click

Or if I'll hear

The same old lies again.

Nothing like that

Nothing so traditional

The fear I have

Is of how good this feels

How easy it is.

And wondering if

I'm going to smother and ruin it.

Or if I allow myself to embrace it.

That's when I'll be ripped from it.

See my fear isn't in

All the bullshit

It's the fear of getting to enjoy and losing it.

[140]

<u>Three lifetimes:</u>

Grateful is too small a word

To describe how much

I owe to you

Indebted more like

Three lifetimes full

With the way you are

And the patience you show

The desire to be you

And for me you grow

To know I am capable

Of being a muse

A catalyst

For a man's personal growth

That's a true stroke of the Ego

To know a glimpse

And be intimate

With his potential

The greatness you are

To you and those around

The life you speak into existence

And the encouragement

Leaves me dumbfounded

So indebted three lifetimes full

To a man who allowed me access

And gave me room

And forgiveness to grow.

[141]

<u>Knightly:</u>

Heaven sent

A gift from actual angels

Lightness you spread

With the way you are

And how that just dances

So softly with who

I am meant

Opening sides of me

You've created a vent

A way to relieve the pressure

I place on myself

Not your burden to carry

But with a smile

You meet me there

In a haven you created

By letting me

Be vulnerable and bare

Knight in shining armor?

More like a personal savior

And it's effortless

Almost second nature

How generously you care.

<u>It's Hard to Say:</u>

It's hard to say it

Sometimes I try

My very hardest

To find ever reason

Not to

But this feeling

Takes over

It overwhelms me

To just grab your face

Pull it in

And scream

I fucking love you.

And you'll roll your eyes

With a smirk

And a sweetly spoken

But I'm just me

See King

It really is that easy

To be loved

Appreciated

Even needed

By queen

Who's healed herself

And again been

healed by you

[143]

<u>A Struggle:</u>

A struggle sometimes to open up

Because a guilt overtakes me

For many reasons

The first of which

If I unburden myself

I'd hate for you to

Hurt, being forced

To be a witness to

my Frustration or suffering

For a man protects

Guides and manages things

So the burden of a woman

To silence herself

To protect his peace is daunting.

The other side of this guilt

Is feeling I'm interrupting

Me giving you what you need

From the softer side of me

But as all double-edged swords swing

The guilt in not sharing,

Even if only occasionally,

Is troubling Because to keep from you

Is holding back a side to me

And if I'm meant to love you correctly

You deserve every part that is me.

Because I know that is the only way

To fairly earn all the parts of you

That need the most nurturing

[144]

<u>Crowded Room:</u>

If I was in a room

Full of men

Had I never met you

I know in my heart

You'd be the one

That I was pulled to

For who you are

My heart craves

Like I've loved you

Through a hundred lifetimes

Like all my past selves

Have laughed and smiled with you

My flesh craves

The touch of your soul

Like it's the only one

Who's learned how

To comfort it correctly.

Your mind and intent

Feels as though

It's memorized

All of my needs

In this lifetime

As well as all the others.

So when I say

If not you it would be

No other

In a room full of men You are the only one

My heart would desire.

[145]

<u>Patience:</u>

Patience with me

Is an absolute must

For as easy as I am,

I come with a but.

She is beautiful but

She doesn't always credit herself as such.

She is smart but

She will always second guess herself.

She is kind but

She has never had that reciprocated

She is soft but

She has only grown in harshness

Her smile is bold and captivating

Her heart is warm and loving

But

She sinks into a sadness

Sometimes she can't be

Saved from

So to love me is to know

You have to watch me struggle

And understand you aren't

Meant to be the buffer.

Patience with me is a must

Simply because

I'm easy to love

But not without

A little sprinkle

of self-doubt.

[146]

<u>Heavenly:</u>

If heaven exists

I'm sure it is

In its entirety

The space

Under your gaze

When you look at me

Like this.

For a want

has never been something

I've seen

For a need

Is only ever what

I've been

But for a soul

To exist

And want who I am

I know I'm not much to look at

But what's inside

Draws you in

Who I am

It's like you crave it

To give me purpose

For all woman

Need to be wanted

Not lusted

But to have purpose

Brings life

For that is the paradise you've created.

[147]

<u>Honestly:</u>

I've only ever been honest

So it baffles me

That I've never spoken on it

That is a man's capacity for love

And this is from learned experiences.

A man is never loved without condition

Therefore

His capacity to love is limited

He may be possessive

Prideful

Even fueled by lust

But the only way

Men can love

Is by loving

The things he created.

His children, job, his status

It's love pride created

This is not a flaw

Just a fact of the matter

So as a woman,

To have purpose

We must accept this

And simply nurture.

For a man's capacity for love

Is built from

The conditions

Under which he suffers.

[148]

Endangered:

Endangered

Because rare is weak

And men like you

Are anything but meek.

Endangered because

There are so few,

Heartless women

Have all but bankrupted you

So my heart is moved to love and protect you

Not from pity, But an understanding

There is a dire need to keep you

Extinction is not an option

Because without men like you

This world will be halted

Better yet haunted

In mourn of what we've done

To strip the motivations

From every last one

To bury them so deep

We forget about the truly great ones

So endangered man

Stay put, give me a little time

To keep us afloat.

Your heart, your character

Is every bit deserving

Of being preserved

Because you see without men like you

Women like me have no meaning.

[149]

<u>Me I Mean:</u>

I am not breath taking

Nor lean

Or really captivating

I never claimed to be

I'm just trying

My damnedest to live laugh love

Unapologetically

For what the world

Took from me

Sewed so many seeds

And from that grew

Extraordinary weeds

But even so

Dandelions are still

kind of pretty

The serve a purpose

And can be interesting

But that being said

I promise you this

I will never need validation

Even to be watered

To further exist.

So I may only be a 5 or a 6

And ahead with looks

I surely won't get

But I'm sturdy

And enduring

And I do serve a fucking purpose.

[150]

<u>Ideally:</u>

The idea of me

Is absolutely captivating

But in reality

I'm flawed fundamentally

In the right ways

For a man

To not be equipped

To want me

Just the idea of me

Not the effort

It takes to keep me

Not the trials

Meant to be persevered

Not the late nights

Trapped in stares

In not knowing

In which way

He's meant to comfort me

The constant battle

Against me

Not seeing my own beauty

So they stay stuck

On What they think I mean

Without the means

To appreciate

The delicacy

That is the softness

Of my vulnerability

[151]

<u>At Times:</u>

Your existence at times

Is simply breath taking

Soul grasping

And earth shaking

To know a truth

There's a realness

I feel in you a greatness untapped

Selfishly I must ask let me keep you

Say your mine

And that I belong to you

For all is fair in love and war

But truthfully, I crave more

To know you, be owned by you

To serve you and so much more

For you have eyes

That speak in kindness

And a smile that wraps tightly

Like a blanket

straight out of the dryer

You are a boldness

That takes over

My more devious senses

And for you

I would knock down

The gates of heaven and hell

Just to know

For a moment

I could be closer to you.

[152]

<u>Ride or Die:</u>

I mean it when I say

I'm not going anywhere

You'd have to

Set fire to the threads

That have our

Souls intwined

And even then

I'd still sweep up the ashes

And try

To retwist them

To sew us back together

I learned long ago

That there's beauty in

Where absence lives

And balance lands

Where someone fills it

Where I love the parts

You don't like so much

And you force my smile

Through all the buts

I could never hide it

Wear my heart

On my sleeve

Because for you

I want it's access

To be easy.

[153]

<u>Chart It, map it, Explore it:</u>

I wanna memorize

Your face

Map it deep

Into my soul

Because I never

want to forget you

I want your image

To disrupt my sleep

And comfort

My every heartbeat

I want to know it

So closely

That I see you

In every new face

I meet and I need that image

To replace

Every single bad memory

To gaze upon you

Makes the butterflies

Grow back new

Makes my heart flutter

And skip to

Its own beat

It's like God sent

An angel just for me

And I would only

Recognize him

The moment my eyes fell on you.

[154]

<u>In Between the Lines:</u>

It's what is left

In what's unsaid

In between the lines

The responses

Laid out in reaction

Not quite a contradiction

But rather Intuition

Caught up in a glance

Or the subtle way

I catch your gaze dance

In the way you

Sink into my words

As the conversations embrace

The soft way

Your hands gravitate

But the firmness

Once they take

Everything to you

That I know I am

Left unsaid

But reassured

Between the words

Time and time again.

<u>Wonder Why:</u>

I often wonder why it is

that good women get

the least of men.

They love the biggest,

but get the least of him.

Left to pick up pieces

of someone she wasn't responsible for breaking.

Of the women in my life like this.

I watch them hang on to scraps

Of what love could be to them.

Or go into hiding

Because to them

The effort in trying

Is always outweighed

by the risk

To be tasked to love

Without conditions

Even to the detriment

To them.

The argument really is

That no one can love

Without condition

If self-love exists.

But good women

Will lose themselves trying

Regardless of what

It does to them.

[156]

<u>Two Souls:</u>

When two souls connect

And it's a balanced

Natural bliss

No fear exists

But in the idea of losing it

The heart ebbs and flows

Amongst the highs and lows

From one moment to the next

And the idea that this moment will be

The one to undo it.

Break us free from the euphoria

We've gotten lost in

This peace we've created

In just two would existing

Two souls healing

Two souls uplifting

Two souls in desperate need of fixing

For who you are

Unappreciated in ways meant to fix me

And who I am

Broken enough to love unconditionally

In the mess you've been given.

So here is to,

Two souls connecting

Whom should have never met

But the world decided

Enough was enough

And mixed them.

[157]

<u>Exhaust Me King:</u>

Exhaust Me King

Full on, dive headfirst

Allow me to be

Relax into this, as you fold into me

Fill me without pause

Open every inch you see

Caress my softness

Let me know

It's me you are devouring

A hunger swells

As you enter me

Be a peace

Both internal and externally

Knees shaking

Look into me

Hush my heavy breathing

I have these intense cravings

To Be your every desire

Like a book

Pour over everyone

of these pages

And for you King

I will submit

Succumb to my urges

Just to please

Push me to limits

Just don't tease.

Turn me into the women of your every fantasy

Rumors:

Simple I may seem

I like wind chimes and house plants but

My heart is not a Stevie Nicks vibe.

My heart is a roller coaster ride where I choke down

snuff out my pride

find my heart.

It's too much Sometimes

I love Big and my soul,

I was told

Its old, but know this

what I've come to

Understand about myself is

I'm not complex.

I'm not complicated.

I'm not difficult or

Too much to manage.

I am a light.

I am a warmth.

I am a kindness.

I am unapologetically me

day or night,

But often, in my mind,

I'm still that scared little girl

The one that stayed up at night, trying not to cry

trying not to blame herself

Trying not to let in

The hateful words that were spilt but I've grown

I've changed

[159]

I've manipulated the things

that were used to manipulate me. I use them as a fuel

to guide me

To be my light to

recharge my energies,

See I'm very simple.

It's almost so easy to be me.

I'm just a nice lady

who likes windchimes

And likes house plants

but I am no Stevie Nicks vibe.

<u>Birthday:</u>

You are a good man

A King in every sense of the word

Kindness and firmness personified

Not only are you a good man.

You are the best kind of man

You are a great man

And I hope you feel as valued

and loved as you should today.

Even though I believe you are worth celebrating every day.

Know that a king and his birthday are meant to be celebrated

A special kind of way.

One of love

Respect

And honor

You are worth celebrating

Yesterday

Today

And tomorrow

Sweet man,

For the love I give comes from a place

Of painful understanding. So for you I will be better than any of them.

~KB~